# YOU CAN
## *Draw*
# FASHIONS

## BY THE EDITORS OF CONSUMER GUIDE®

Publications International, Ltd.

# Contents

Louis Weber, C.E.O.
Publications International, Ltd.
7373 North Cicero Avenue
Lincolnwood, Illinois 60646

8 7 6 5 4 3 2 1

ISBN 1-56173-110-2

Illustrator: Ilene Robinette

# Introduction

The easy, step-by-step instructions on the following pages can turn you into an artist. Anyone can do it.

All you need is a No. 2 pencil, a pencil sharpener, and an eraser. Then use *You Can Draw Fashions* to practice drawing men, women, and children wearing various types of fashions.

Each drawing begins with a few simple shapes printed in red ink. The second step shows the first drawing in black. The new shapes and marks you're going to add appear in red. This shows you how to make step one's drawing look like that in step two. The following steps also show the earlier drawings in black and the new marks and shapes in red.

Blank space near each step lets you practice your drawing skills. You can also compare your drawing with the printed one. Draw lightly with your pencil. This makes it easier to erase mistakes and other marks that change slightly in later steps. When you have finished, use a pen or fine felt-tip marker to darken the pencil marks that make up the finished drawing. Then gently erase any remaining pencil marks.

When you are done, you will have 17 drawings showing people wearing all kinds of fashions.

If you wish, you can add color by using crayons or colored pencils or markers. You may want to cut out your drawings and tape or glue them onto colored construction paper. Then you will be able to display your collection of drawings showing all sorts of fashions. Have fun.

# Little Girl with a Picnic Basket

**1** Sketch an oval for the head. Divide the oval into left and right halves with a vertical line to determine the center of the face. Separate the oval into upper and lower halves with a horizontal line to show the position of the tops of the eyes. Sketch a horizontal line for the hairline about one-sixth of the way down from the top of the oval. Divide the area below that into three equal parts. The first line below the hairline is for the eyebrows, and the next line shows the location of the tip of the nose. The ears lie between the eyebrows and the nose.

Divide the area below the nose into three more equal parts. The line below the nose is for the mouth opening, and the next line is for the lower lip.

Draw a curved line under the head to show the shape of the neck and backbone. Use rectangles for the chest and hip areas. Form the arms and legs with curved tube shapes. Sketch oval shapes for the shoulders. Draw a circle for the hand area and two small circles for the kneecaps. Use wedge shapes for the feet. Draw a rectangle to form the picnic basket under and to the left of the thighs.

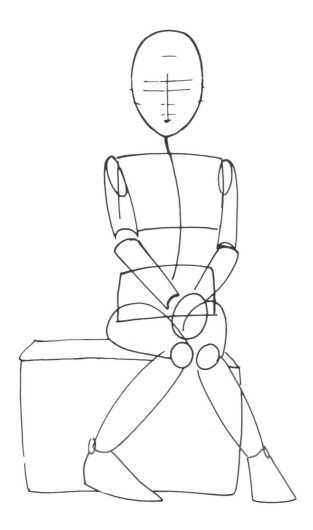

4

**2** Draw two small ovals to shape the ears. Use rounded lines to form the hairline and a U-shaped figure for the jaw. Shape the neck and shoulders with curved lines. Extend the curved lines for the arms and hands. Block the hat with long curved lines. Draw more curved lines to shape the clothes.

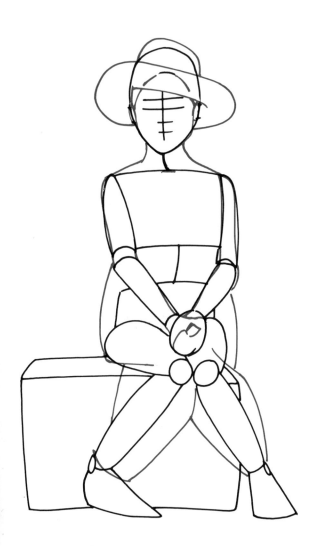

*Use a pen on the final drawing; then erase pencil marks.*

# Little Girl with a Picnic Basket continued

**3** Use short curved lines to draw in the eyes and eyebrows. Form the nose with short straight lines and shape the mouth with full lips as shown here. Use straight lines for the collar and the folds in the clothes. Draw a bow with curved lines. Use two long straight lines to draw the handle of the basket; connect the two lines with a short curve. Use three odd-shaped triangles for the cloth that is peeking out of the picnic basket. Draw a curved line to add a band to the hat. Start shaping the fingers with small banana-shaped figures. Smooth out the shoes with long rounded lines.

*For each step, draw lightly with your pencil.*

**4** Add squiggles to the clothes to show wrinkles and folds. Extend curved shapes from the lower left of the hat for the scarf. Add several long wavy lines for the hair. Form the sandals with straight lines and triangles. Draw squares all over the basket. Do the same with the cloth peeking out of the basket, but remember to follow its shape. Use blackened ovals to draw in the eyes.

# Little Girl with a Picnic Basket continued

**5** Draw thick straight lines on the hat, chin, collar,
bow, hands, and feet for shading. Add two
small horizontal lines to every other square in the
basket; fill in the remaining squares with two short
vertical lines. Blacken in every other square in the
cloth. Use many straight short lines to add the
weave to the hat as shown.

*For each step, draw lightly with your pencil.*

# Little Girl in a Fairy Costume

**1** Sketch a tipped oval for the head. Divide the oval into uneven left and right halves with a vertical line to determine the center of the face. Separate the oval into upper and lower halves with a horizontal line to show the position of the tops of the eyes. Sketch a horizontal line for the hairline about one-sixth of the way down from the top of the oval. Divide the area below that into three equal parts. The first line below the hairline is for the eyebrows, and the next line shows the location of the tip of the nose. The ears lie between the eyebrows and the nose. Divide the area below the nose into three more equal parts. The line below

the nose is for the mouth opening, and the next line is for the lower lip.

Draw a straight line under the head to show the shape of the neck and backbone. Use rectangles for the chest and hip areas. Form the arms and legs with curved tube shapes. Add ovals to shape the shoulders and kneecaps. Draw a short horizontal line between the chest and hip rectangles to mark the waist. Shape the left hand in an oval shape and the right hand in a diamond shape. Use wedge shapes for the feet. Draw in a long straight line for the wand in the left hand and top it with a star.

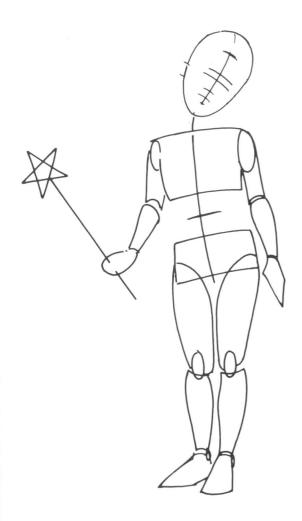

*Use a pen on the final drawing; then erase pencil marks.*

**2** Draw a V-shaped figure over a U-shaped figure. Connect the two shapes with short straight lines to form the hat. Use small oval shapes to form the ears. Establish the jawline with a U-shaped figure. Extend curved lines from the jawline down to the shoulders and arms. Smooth out the legs with slightly curved lines. Shape the hands as shown here.

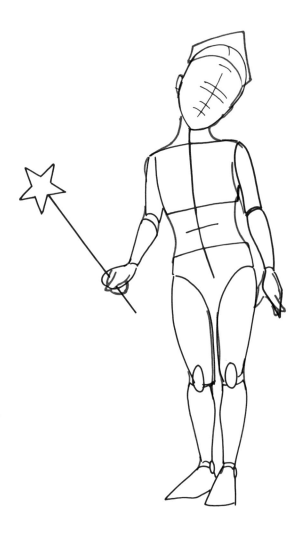

*For each step, draw lightly with your pencil.*

**3** Shape the hair with long curved lines. Add the eyes and eyebrows with short curved lines. Use short straight lines for the nose. Form the lips with thick curved lines. Use odd-shaped ovals and triangles for the sleeves. Draw a straight line across the chest for the neckline. Add two curved lines for the sides and an incomplete triangle for the skirt. Smooth the fingers and shoes with curved lines.

*Use a pen on the final drawing; then erase pencil marks.*

# Little Girl in a Fairy Costume continued

**4** Finish the eyes with ovals. Use zigzag lines to shape the crown. Form the wings with two oval shapes. Extend them over the shoulders and under the elbows. Draw horizontal lines at the waist, bodice, and shoes to shape the ruffles. Add many straight lines to the skirt and hem to show the folds and uneven hem. Shape the sleeves with a few scribbles. Shade the star and draw a ribbon on the wand as shown.

*For each step, draw lightly with your pencil.*

**5** Shade the hair with dark curved lines. Add lacy scribbles to the crown and bodice. Draw long straight lines from the sleeves to the outer parts of the wings. Add shading to the wand, shoes, and skirt.

# Boy in a Pirate Costume

**1** Sketch an oval shape for the head. Divide the oval into left and right halves with a vertical line to determine the center of the face. Separate the oval into upper and lower halves with a horizontal line to show the position of the tops of the eyes. Sketch a horizontal line for the hairline about one-sixth of the way down from the top of the oval. Divide the area below that into three equal parts. The first line below the hairline is for the eyebrows, and the next line shows the location of the nose.

The ears lie between the eyebrows and the nose. Divide the area below the nose into three more equal parts. The line below the nose is for the mouth opening, and the next line is for the lower lip.

Draw a straight line under the head to show the shape of the neck and backbone. Use rectangles for the chest and hip areas. Form the arms and legs with curved tube shapes. Use ovals to mark the shoulders and kneecaps. Draw in a line for the waist. Use wedge shapes for the hands and feet.

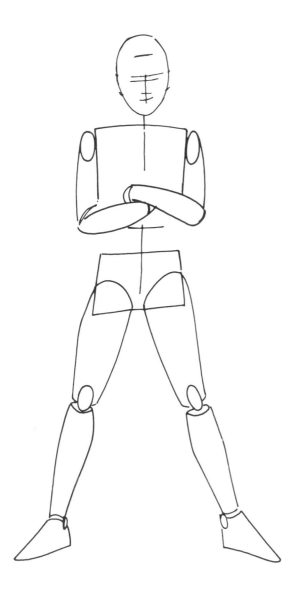

14

**2** Use small ovals to draw in the ears. Mark the hairline with oval lines. Shape the hat with an odd-shaped triangle and an oval. Use a U-shaped figure to draw in the jawline, extending it with curved lines to the shoulders. Smooth out the legs with long straight lines. Use two slightly curved lines to draw in the sash.

*Use a pen on the final drawing; then erase pencil marks.*

# Boy in a Pirate Costume continued

**3** Draw the eye and eyebrow with short curved lines. Use short straight lines for the nose. Add two short squiggles for the sides of the mouth. Sketch the headband with a dark straight line as shown. Draw a half-circle underneath for the patch. Use a long V-shape for the neckline and long U-shapes for the full sleeves. Draw two curved lines for the cuffs on the sleeves. Add a few curved lines near the arms and under the chin. Draw a rounded shape for the sword grip and two long curved lines that join at the bottom for the blade. Use curved lines for the cuffs on the boots. Give the legs shape with long straight lines.

*For each step, draw lightly with your pencil.*

**4** Finish the eye with a blackened oval. Add more folds and wrinkles to the hat, sleeves, and boots with long straight lines. Draw in the scarf as shown. Add a collar to the shirt with L-shaped and straight lines. Detail the belt with long rectangular shapes. Use circles and curves to mark the sword grip. Form the zipper area with two straight lines and a bent line.

*Use a pen on the final drawing; then erase pencil marks.*

# Boy in a Pirate Costume continued

**5** Fill in the patch, belt, and vest. Draw in a button on the shirt and another on the cuff. Add shading to the hat as shown. Shade the sword. Add squiggles to the boots to show wrinkles and shading.

*For each step, draw lightly with your pencil.*

# Teenage Girl in a Blazer and Shorts

**1** Sketch a tipped oval for the head. Divide the oval into left and right halves with a vertical line to determine the center of the face. Separate the oval into upper and lower halves with a horizontal line to show the position of the tops of the eyes. Sketch a horizontal line for the hairline about one-sixth of the way down from the top of the oval. Divide the area below that into three equal parts. The first line below the hairline is for the eyebrows, and the next line shows the location of the tip of the nose. The ears lie between the eyebrows and the nose. Divide the area below the nose into three more equal parts. The line below the nose is for the mouth opening, and the next line is for the lower lip.

Draw a curved line under the head to show the shape of the neck and backbone. Use rectangles for the chest and hip areas. Draw a line between the two rectangles for the waist. Form the arms and legs with curved tube shapes. Sketch oval shapes for the shoulders, knees, and ankles. Use wedge shapes for the feet.

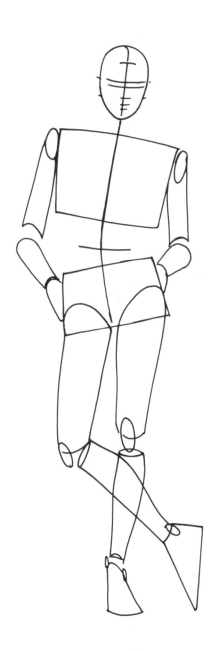

*Use a pen on the final drawing; then erase pencil marks.*

# Teenage Girl in a Blazer and Shorts continued

**2** Draw two small ovals for the ears. Block the hat with an odd-shaped rectangle. Use an incomplete oval for the hairline and the outline of the face. Extend two long curved lines from the jawline to form the shoulders. Draw in the shape of the sleeves and shorts with long bent lines. Smooth out the legs and ankles with curved lines.

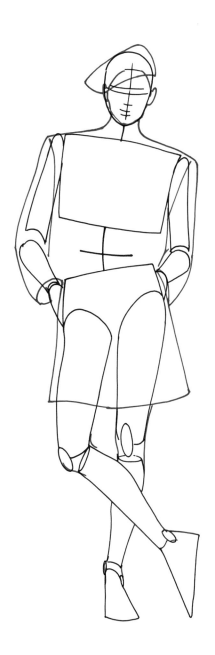

*For each step, draw lightly with your pencil.*

**3** Use small curved lines for the eyebrows. Draw ovals with pointed ends for the eyes. Form the nose with short straight lines. Add the mouth with odd-shaped ovals as shown. Use longer curved lines for the hair and bangs. Add a V-shaped figure under the neck for the neckline. Draw an oval underneath it. Use long triangles for the lapels and curved lines for the sleeves and shape of the blazer. Draw an uneven horizontal line for the waistband of the sweater. Sketch the zipper area with one straight line and one bent line that connect halfway. Use more straight lines to form the shorts. Shape the shoes with curved lines.

*Use a pen on the final drawing; then erase pencil marks.*

# Teenage Girl in a Blazer and Shorts continued

**4** Finish the eyes with darkened ovals. Use curved lines to shape the beret. Sketch odd-shaped rectangles for the bow. Add details to the blazer with curved lines and squiggles. Draw straight lines from the waistband to form pleats.

Add zigzag lines for the wrinkles. Draw two uneven lines on the bottom of the shorts to form cuffs. Shape the kneecap with a small line. Form the shoes with V-shaped and U-shaped figures.

*For each step, draw lightly with your pencil.*

**5** Use squiggles to finish the hair. Detail the fringe on the scarf with short straight lines. Add straight horizontal and vertical lines for the pattern on the sweater as shown. Use vertical lines for the ribbing on the left sleeve and the bottom of the sweater. Finish the shoes with curved lines. Shade the neck, jacket, shorts, and legs.

*Use a pen on the final drawing; then erase pencil marks.*

# Teenage Girl in a Vogue Outfit

**1** Sketch an oval for the head. Divide the oval into left and right halves with a vertical line to determine the center of the face. Separate the oval into upper and lower halves with a horizontal line to show the position of the tops of the eyes. Sketch a horizontal line for the hairline about one-sixth of the way down from the top of the oval. Divide the area below that into three equal parts. The first line below the hairline is for the eyebrows, and the next line shows the location of the tip of the nose. The ears lie between the eyebrows and the nose.

Divide the area below the nose into three more equal parts. The line below the nose is for the mouth opening, and the next line is for the lower lip.

Draw a curved line under the head to show the shape of the neck and backbone. Use rectangles for the chest and hip areas. Add a line between the rectangles for the waist. Form the arms and legs with curved tube shapes. Sketch oval shapes for the shoulders and kneecaps. Use wedge shapes for the feet.

*For each step, draw lightly with your pencil.*

**2** Draw ovals for the ears. Use a U-shaped figure to form the jawline. Extend a curved line from the neck to form the shoulders. Block the shape of the hat using an odd-shaped rectangle. Draw in the shape of the sleeves and skirt with long straight lines. Smooth out the ankles with short straight lines.

*Use a pen on the final drawing; then erase pencil marks.*

# Teenage Girl in a Vogue Outfit continued

**3** Use two curves for the eyebrows. Add two ovals with pointed ends for the shape of the eyes. Draw the nose with straight lines. Form the mouth with an odd-shaped oval as shown. Sketch the hair with long wavy lines. Use triangles to shape the collar of the blouse. Draw the collar of the jacket with two long connecting triangles. Use a straight line to form the opening of the jacket. Draw the bottom of the jacket with straight lines. Add two straight lines to the sides of the jacket for pockets. Extend bent lines from the bottom of the jacket to the hem. Use these folds to draw the hemline. Draw short curves to form the leggings, socks, and boots.

26

**4** Finish the eyes with darkened ovals. Add wavy lines to the hair and hat. Sketch a placket on the front of the blouse using two straight vertical lines. Use curved lines to shape the sleeves. Add a pocket to the breast of the jacket with a rectangle. Form a handkerchief on top of it with wavy lines.

Add two other pockets on the sides of the jacket using straight lines. Sketch two buttons on the jacket. Use straight lines to add folds to the skirt. Draw a wavy horizontal line on the bottom of the skirt for detail. Shape the boots with bent lines.

*Use a pen on the final drawing; then erase pencil marks.*

**5** Shade the hair with squiggles. Add two straight horizontal lines to the bridge of the nose. Draw different-shaped buttons on the blouse and shade them. Use curly lines to detail the handkerchief. Shade the jacket and skirt. Draw laces on the boots with small ovals.

*For each step, draw lightly with your pencil.*

# Man in a Tuxedo

**1** Sketch a tipped oval for the head. Divide the oval into uneven left and right halves with a vertical line to determine the center of the face. Separate the oval into upper and lower halves with a horizontal line to show the position of the tops of the eyes. Sketch a horizontal line for the hairline about one-sixth of the way down from the top of the oval. Divide the area below that into three equal parts. The first line below the hairline is for the eyebrows, and the next line shows the location of the tip of the nose. The ears lie between the eyebrows and the nose. Divide the area below the nose into three more equal parts. The line below the nose is for the mouth opening, and the next line is for the lower lip.

Draw a curved line under the head to show the shape of the neck and backbone. Use rectangles for the chest and hip areas. Form the right arm and legs with curved tube shapes. Use ovals for the shoulder, kneecap, and ankles. Draw an odd-shaped rectangle for the hand. Use wedge shapes for the feet.

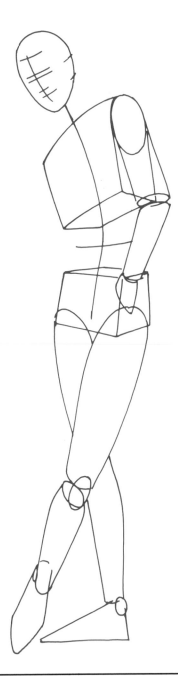

*Use a pen on the final drawing; then erase pencil marks.*

# Man in a Tuxedo continued

**2** Draw an oval shape for the ear. Frame the face and hairline with an odd-shaped oval. Extend two long curved lines from the bottom of the head to form the shoulders. Continue the same lines below the shoulders to form the arms. Use odd-shaped triangles for the left arm and hand. Shape the slacks with long straight lines.

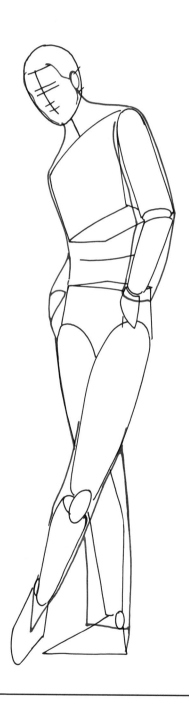

*For each step, draw lightly with your pencil.*

**3** Sketch several long curved lines to shape the hair. Add a squiggle inside the ear. Use dark curved shapes for the eyebrows and ovals with pointed ends for the eyes. Form the nose with an L-shaped figure and a comma-shaped figure. Draw a larger oval with pointed ends for the mouth. Fill in the bottom part of the mouth as shown. Draw a curved line under the mouth for the chin crease. Use a long U-shape for the neckline. Draw two rounded triangles underneath. Connect them with a small oval to form the bow tie. Shape two long tube shapes for the lapels. Draw two horizontal lines near the bottom of the lapels for the cummerbund. Extend a vertical line perpendicular to the bottom of the cummerbund for the zipper area. Add a small curved line for the right pocket. Use two incomplete triangles for the cut of the jacket. Add a few long straight lines to the slacks to show wrinkles.

*Use a pen on the final drawing; then erase pencil marks.*

# Man in a Tuxedo continued

**4** Finish the eyes with darkened ovals. Add a curly line and straight line to the right of the nose for the smile creases. Sketch lines right below both shoulders for the seams. Add two squiggles on the bow tie for wrinkles. Shade the right-hand side of the bow tie. Draw a T-shaped figure to shape the jacket collar. Add a pocket to the jacket with two straight parallel lines connected at the right tip. Use zigzag lines for wrinkles on the right sleeve. Draw horizontal lines on the cummerbund for pleats and a straight line on each side of the jacket for wrinkles. Use a straight line for the crease in the slacks, and several curved lines to outline the shoes.

*For each step, draw lightly with your pencil.*

**5** Add many scribbles to the hair. Shade the neck, chin, jacket, and slacks. Draw small buttons on the shirt and three larger oval buttons on the right sleeve. Add a few details to the shoes.

*Use a pen on the final drawing; then erase pencil marks.*

# Man in a Casual Sweater

**1** Sketch an egg for the head. Divide the egg into uneven left and right halves with a vertical line to determine the center of the face. Separate the egg into upper and lower halves with a horizontal line to show the position of the tops of the eyes. Sketch a horizontal line for the hairline about one-sixth of the way down from the top of the oval. Divide the area below that into three equal parts. The first line below the hairline is for the eyebrows, and the next line shows the location of the tip of the nose. The ears lie between the eyebrows and the nose. Divide the area below the nose into three more equal parts. The line below the nose is for the mouth opening, and the next line is for the lower lip.

Draw a curved line under the head to show the shape of the neck and backbone. Use rectangles for the chest and hip areas. Form the arms with curved tube shapes. Use oval shapes to form the shoulders. Draw partial rectangles for the hands.

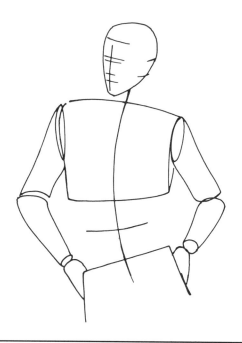

*For each step, draw lightly with your pencil.*

**2** Draw in an oval shape for the ear. Use curved lines to establish the shape of the face and the hairline. Sketch a U-shaped figure for the jawline. Extend two curved lines from both sides of the head for the shoulders and arms. Sketch in the sides of the sweater. Use two odd-shaped ovals to separate the sides from the arms.

**3** Shape the hair with curved lines. Draw in two dark curves for the eyebrows. Form the eyes with dark ovals. Use an L-shaped figure and a comma-shaped figure for the nose. Draw full lips as shown. Use curved lines to form the collar of the turtleneck sweater. Sketch V-shaped figures to form the collar of the V-necked sweater. Draw a slightly curved line for the left shoulder. Separate the body of the sweater from the sleeves and waistband with bent lines. Draw in many curved lines to show the wrinkles.

*Use a pen on the final drawing; then erase pencil marks.*

# Man in a Casual Sweater continued

**4** Draw lines on the V-necked sweater to form diamond shapes. Add pleats to the pants with straight lines. Use curved lines to form wrinkles on the sleeves of the sweater.

**5** Use short squiggles to finish the hair. Add a dark line on the jaw for shading. Use many short straight lines on the collar of the turtleneck sweater to show ribbing. Add more ribbing to the neckline, cuffs, and waistband of the V-necked sweater. Fill in every other diamond on the V-necked sweater with straight up-and-down lines to define the knit.

*For each step, draw lightly with your pencil.*

# Man in a Bomber Jacket

**1** Sketch an oval for the head. Divide the oval into uneven left and right halves with a vertical line to determine the center of the face. Separate the oval into upper and lower halves with a horizontal line to show the position of the tops of the eyes. Sketch a horizontal line for the hairline about one-sixth of the way down from the top of the oval. Divide the area below that into three equal parts. The first line below the hairline is for the eyebrows, and the next line shows the location of the tip of the nose. The ears lie between the eyebrows and the nose. Divide the area below the nose into three more equal parts. The line below the nose is for the mouth opening, and the next line is for the lower lip.

Draw a curved line under the head to show the shape of the neck and backbone. Use rectangles for the chest and hip areas. Add a line between the two rectangles for the waist. Form the arms with curved tube shapes. Use ovals to shape the shoulders. Draw odd-shaped rectangles for the hands. Sketch odd-shaped U-figures for the legs.

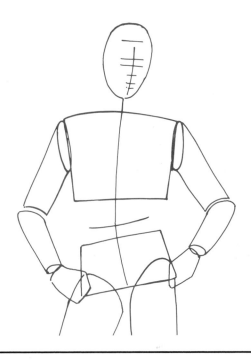

*Use a pen on the final drawing; then erase pencil marks.*

# Man in a Bomber Jacket continued

**2** Shape the hairline with a slightly curved line at the top of the head and two curved lines at each side as shown. Draw the ears with oval shapes. Establish the jawline with a U-shaped figure. Extend long curved lines from the jawline to shape the shoulders and arms. Use two slightly curved lines for the sides of the jacket. Sketch straight lines to shape the slacks.

**3** Use squiggles to shape the hair. Draw two ovals over the eyes and connect them to form the sunglasses. Use odd-shaped triangles to shape the collar of the jacket and the collar of the shirt. Extend a line from the collar of the shirt to the waist to show the opening. Add another straight horizontal line below the waist to form the belt. Use E-shapes to draw the fingers. Add a few straight lines in the jacket and slacks to show wrinkles.

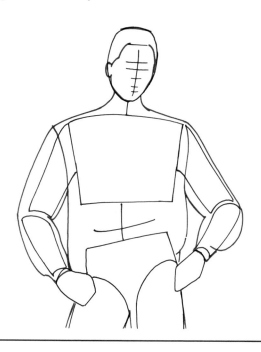

*For each step, draw lightly with your pencil.*

**4** Draw in a short straight line from the glasses to the left ear. Use triangles to shape the jacket and shirt collars. Add short lines beneath the shoulders and on the right side of the jacket opening for seams. Sketch many straight and curved lines to the sleeves, slacks, and shirt to establish wrinkles. Use rectangles to draw pockets for the jacket and slacks. Draw a small oval and a small rectangle on the belt to shape the buckle. Use three straight lines to show the zipper area.

**5** Add hair with curly lines. Shade in the lenses of the sunglasses. Draw in round buttons on the shirt. Show shading in the jacket with thick black lines as shown. Add many squiggles to the jacket to show wrinkles. Outline the pockets on the jacket to give them finishing touches. Add ribbing to the bottom of the jacket and the sleeves with short straight lines.

*Use a pen on the final drawing; then erase pencil marks.*

# Rock Star

1 Sketch an oval for the head. Divide the oval into left and right halves with a vertical line to determine the center of the face. Separate the oval into upper and lower halves with a horizontal line to show the position of the tops of the eyes. Sketch a horizontal line for the hairline about one-sixth of the way down from the top of the oval. Divide the area below that into three equal parts. The first line below the hairline is for the eyebrows, and the next line shows the location of the tip of the nose. The ears lie between the eyebrows and the nose. Divide the area below the nose into three more equal parts. The line below the nose is for the mouth opening, and the next line is for the lower lip.

Draw a straight line under the head to show the shape of the neck and backbone. Use a rectangle for the chest area. Form the arms and legs with curved tube shapes. Use ovals to shape the shoulders, right hand, and kneecaps. Draw the left hand with an odd-shaped rectangle. Sketch the shape of an electric guitar. Put the neck of the guitar next to the hands. Add a curved line for the waist just above the top of the guitar.

*For each step, draw lightly with your pencil.*

**2** Draw ovals for the ears. Sketch two curved lines on the head to form a headband. Form the shape of the face, neck, and shoulders with curved lines. Add lines across the upper arms for the sleeves. Block the arms and legs with long straight and curved lines. Add lines to the sides of the chest. Sketch in guitar details as shown.

*Use a pen on the final drawing; then erase pencil marks.*

**3** Use curved lines to form the hair. Add dark curves for the eyebrows and lighter curves underneath them for the eyes. Draw straight and curved lines for the nose. Use an outlined oval for the mouth. Form the collar of the vest and the neckline of the shirt with curved lines. Add straight lines on the sleeves. Draw a squiggle on the neck. Detail the guitar to add depth. Shape the fingers with odd-shaped ovals.

*For each step, draw lightly with your pencil.*

**4** Add details to the headband. Finish the eyes with darkened ovals. Add a curly line in the left ear. Shape indentations in the collar and edges of the vest. Draw the shoulder strap using straight lines. Add wrinkles to the shirt. Draw three ovals on each side of the head of the guitar. Continue detailing the guitar as shown.

*Use a pen on the final drawing; then erase pencil marks.*

# Rock Star

**5** Shade the hair with short squiggles. Outline the collar with V-shaped figures and add wrinkles to the top of the shirt. Add tiny lines to the edges of the vest collar and sleeves to make them look like zipper teeth. Finish detailing the guitar. Shade the edges of the vest and guitar as shown.

*For each step, draw lightly with your pencil.*

# Woman in a Sundress

**1** Sketch an oval for the head. Divide the oval into uneven left and right halves with a vertical line to determine the center of the face. Separate the oval into upper and lower halves with a horizontal line to show the position of the tops of the eyes. Sketch a horizontal line for the hairline one-sixth of the way down from the top of the oval. Divide the area below that into three equal parts. The first line below the hairline is for the eyebrows, and the next line shows the location of the tip of the nose. The ears lie between the eyebrows and the nose. Divide the area below the nose into three more equal parts. The line below the nose is for the mouth opening, and the next line is for the lower lip.

Draw a curved line under the head to show the shape of the neck and backbone. Use rectangles for the chest and hip areas. Form the arms and legs with curved tube shapes. Sketch oval shapes for the shoulders and kneecaps. Draw two odd-shaped diamonds for the hands. Use wedge shapes for the feet.

*Use a pen on the final drawing; then erase pencil marks.*

# Woman in a Sundress continued

**2** Draw two small ovals to form the ears. Use curved lines above and below the ears for the hairline. Add ovals to block the hat. Extend curved lines below the hat for the neck and shoulders. Draw in straight lines for the bodice. Use small curved lines to shape the chin, right elbow and wrist, and ankles. Sketch curved and wavy lines to define the skirt.

*For each step, draw lightly with your pencil.*

**3** Use squiggles at the temples for the hair. Add a slightly curved line below the brim of the hat for the bangs. Draw in the ears, eyes, mouth, and hair with curves and ovals as shown. Sketch a V-shaped figure for the neckline and a set of straight lines for each shoulder strap. Extend two lines from the shoulder straps below the waist. Draw an odd-shaped V at the end of these lines. Sketch several long straight lines from the V-shape to the hem. Make sure the hem of the skirt flows with the folds. Use odd-shaped rectangles and triangles to form the shoes. Shape the hands with curved lines.

*Use a pen on the final drawing; then erase pencil marks.*

# Woman in a Sundress continued

**4** Darken in the eyes and use dark curves for the eyebrows. Add zigzag lines at the top of the bodice and curved lines at the hemline. Show the waistline with two small horizontal lines. Add many squiggles to the skirt to show wrinkles. Use odd-shaped ovals for the bracelets.

*For each step, draw lightly with your pencil.*

**5** Finish the hair with squiggles. Add texture to the hat with short straight lines. Draw horizontal lines on the bodice of the dress. Add shading to the side, bracelets, and skirt.

# Walking Woman in a Pantsuit

**1** Draw an egg for the head. Divide the egg into uneven left and right halves with a vertical line to determine the center of the face. Separate the egg into upper and lower halves with a horizontal line for the hairline about one-sixth of the way down from the top of the egg. Divide the area below that into three equal parts. The first line below the hairline is for the eyebrows, and the next line shows the location of the tip of the nose. The ears lie between the eyebrows and the nose. Divide the area below the nose into three more equal parts.

The line below the nose is for the mouth opening, and the next line is for the lower lip.

Draw a curved line under the head to show the shape of the neck and backbone. Use rectangles for the chest and hip areas. Draw a curved line between the two rectangles to determine the waist. Form the arms and legs with curved tube shapes. Sketch oval shapes for the right shoulder, kneecaps, and ankles. Use wedge shapes for the feet. Draw a diamond shape for the left hand and an odd-shaped oval for the right hand.

*For each step, draw lightly with your pencil.*

**2** Draw an oval for the ear. Extend lines above it for the hairline and below it for the neck. Block in the shape of the hat with odd-shaped triangles and ovals. Sketch the shape of the jacket and slacks with long straight lines. Add the shawl with long straight and curved lines.

*Use a pen on the final drawing; then erase pencil marks.*

# Walking Woman in a Pantsuit continued

**3** Use long curved lines for the hair and ovals with pointed ends for the eyes. Draw the nose and lips with curved lines as shown. Sketch a very short line at the chin for definition. Shape the jacket and shawl with long squiggles. Add two pockets to the jacket with rectangles. Form the hands with curved lines. Draw in the shape of the boots with straight lines.

*For each step, draw lightly with your pencil.*

**4** Finish the eyes with darkened ovals. Sketch a curved line on the hat for the ribbon. Add an E-shaped figure to the left side of the lips for definition. Sketch squiggles on the jacket and slacks to show wrinkles. Add a border to the shawl.

*Use a pen on the final drawing; then erase pencil marks.*

# Walking Woman in a Pantsuit continued

**5** Finish the hair with squiggles. Add shading to the hat, jacket, and boots. Draw three oval buttons on the bottom of the right jacket sleeve. Finish the shawl with straight lines to define the fringe.

*For each step, draw lightly with your pencil.*

# Woman in an Oversize Sweater

**1** Sketch an oval for the head. Divide the oval into uneven left and right halves with a vertical line to determine the center of the face. Separate the oval into upper and lower halves with a horizontal line to show the position of the tops of the eyes. Sketch a horizontal line for the hairline about one-sixth of the way down from the top of the oval. Divide the area below that into three equal parts. The first line below the hairline is for the eyebrows, and the next line shows the location of the tip of the nose. The ears lie between the eyebrows and the nose. Divide the area below the nose into three more equal parts. The line below the nose is for the mouth opening, and the next line is for the lower lip.

Draw a curved line under the head to show the shape of the neck and backbone. Use rectangles for the chest and hip areas. Add a line between the two rectangles for the waist. Sketch oval shapes for the shoulders.

# Woman in an Oversize Sweater continued

**2** Draw a small oval for the right ear. Use curved lines for the hairline and an uneven line for the shape of the face. Add long curved lines from the shoulders to shape the sleeves. Draw the sweater and legs with long curved lines.

**3** Use two small curves for the eyebrows. Draw ovals with pointed ends for the eyes. Use straight lines for the nose. Add two odd-shaped curves for the lips as shown. Use long wavy lines for the hair, cuffs of the sweater, and fingers. Form wrinkles in the sleeves with squiggles. Detail the belt with curved lines as shown.

*For each step, draw lightly with your pencil.*

**4** Finish the eyes with blackened ovals. Add wrinkles to the sweater with zigzag lines. Sketch in the details of the belt with rectangles and triangles. Add folds to the sweater to form an uneven hemline.

**5** Finish the hair with squiggles. Draw a short curved line on the upper lip for definition. Use ovals for the earrings. Add shading to the sweater and legs for depth.

*Use a pen on the final drawing; then erase pencil marks.*

# Woman in a Bathing Suit

**1** Sketch an egg for the head. Divide the egg into uneven left and right halves with a vertical line to determine the center of the face. Separate the egg into upper and lower halves with a horizontal line to show the position of the tops of the eyes. Sketch a horizontal line for the hairline about one-sixth of the way down from the top of the head. Divide the area below that into three equal parts. The first line below the hairline is for the eyebrows, and the next line shows the location of the tip of the nose. The ears lie between the eyebrows and the nose. Divide the area below the nose into three more equal parts. The line below the nose is for the mouth opening, and the next line is for the lower lip.

Draw a curved line under the head to show the shape of the neck and backbone. Use rectangles for the chest and hip areas. Form the arms and legs with curved tube shapes. Add a curved line between the two rectangles for the waist. Sketch oval shapes for the shoulders and kneecaps. Use odd-shaped V-figures for the hands. Block the feet with wedge shapes.

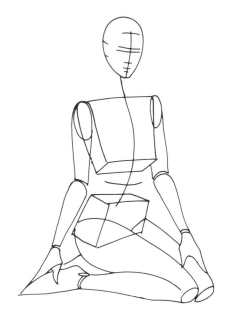

*For each step, draw lightly with your pencil.*

**2** Draw an oval for the ear. Use curved lines to define the hairline and jawline. Extend long curved lines from the head for the neck and shoulders. Smooth out the arms, hands, and shoes with slightly curved lines. Define the torso with two curved lines.

**3** Draw the head scarf with odd-shaped triangles and rectangles. Use long curved lines to shape the hair. Sketch curved lines for the eyebrows and ovals with pointed ends for the eyes. Form the nose and lips with straight and curved lines as shown. Use V-shapes to define the neck and the neckline of the bathing suit. Add odd-shaped V-figures to define the fingers and shoes.

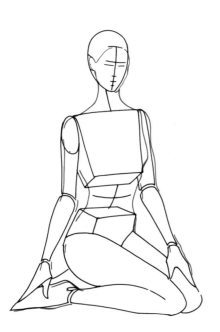

*Use a pen on the final drawing; then erase pencil marks.*

# Woman in a Bathing Suit continued

**4** Use darkened ovals to finish the eyes and dark curves for the eyelids. Add squiggles to the head scarf to show wrinkles. Draw odd-shaped flowers on the bathing suit.

**5** Add squiggles to finish the head scarf and hair. Draw thin lines on the bathing suit to fill in the pattern. Darken the shoes and add shading to the knee.

*For each step, draw lightly with your pencil.*

# Woman in a Fashionable Topcoat

**1** Sketch an egg for the head. Divide the egg into uneven left and right halves with a vertical line to determine the center of the face. Separate the egg into upper and lower halves with a horizontal line to show the position of the tops of the eyes. Sketch a horizontal line for the hairline about one-sixth of the way down from the top of the head. Divide the area below that into three equal parts. The first line below the hairline is for the eyebrows, and the next line shows the location of the tip of the nose. The ears lie between the eyebrows and the nose. Divide the area below the nose into three more equal parts. The line below the nose is for the mouth opening, and the next line is for the lower lip.

Draw a curved line under the head to show the shape of the neck and backbone. Use rectangles for the chest and hip areas. Add a line between the rectangles for the waist. Form the arms and legs with curved tube shapes. Sketch oval shapes for the shoulders, kneecap, and ankles. Draw odd-shaped rectangles for the hands and feet.

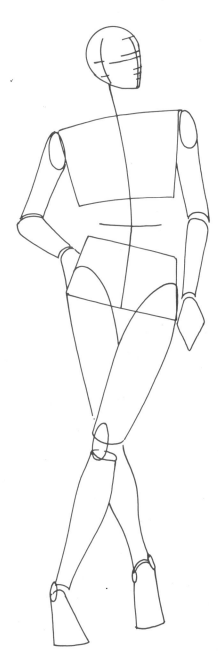

*Use a pen on the final drawing; then erase pencil marks.*

**2** Block the hat with rectangles and ovals. Shape the profile of the face with a curly line. Draw the neck with curved lines and extend them to form the shoulders. Sketch a U-shaped figure for the neckline. Use long straight lines to shape the coat and slacks. Add a short straight line to form the hand.

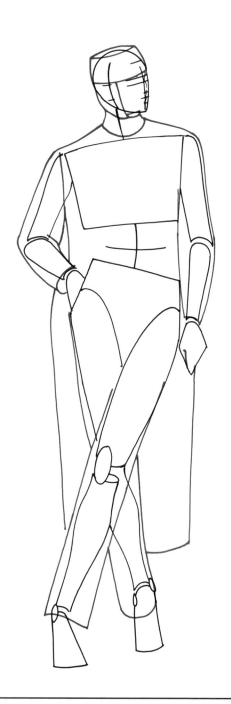

*For each step, draw lightly with your pencil.*

**3** Draw in a curved line for the eyebrows and an oval with pointed edges for the eye. Shape the nose with an L-shaped line and a straight line. Draw a full mouth as shown. Add uneven lines to give the hat shape. Use two curved lines for the sweater collar and two triangles for the coat collar. Shape the coat and slacks with long straight lines. Draw a curved line for the bottom of the sweater. Shape the shoes with curved lines. Add several short lines to the sleeves, sweater, and slacks to show folds. Draw the hand with curved lines as shown.

*Use a pen on the final drawing; then erase pencil marks.*

**4** Finish the eyes with blackened ovals and the eyelids with V-shapes. Add two small curves on the top of the hat for shading. Use squiggles on the collar, coat, and slacks for folds and wrinkles. Sketch zigzag lines to form the gloves in the right hand. Use V-shapes for the shoes.

*For each step, draw lightly with your pencil.*

**5** Add zigzag lines over the coat, slacks, and
sweater for wrinkles. Shade the collar, coat,
gloves, and slacks. Add three round buttons to the
right side of the coat. Draw a wavy line at mid-
chest for detail.

# Woman in a Cocktail Dress

**1** Draw an oval with a pointed lower left side for the head. Divide the oval into uneven left and right halves with a vertical line to determine the center of the head. Separate the oval into upper and lower halves with a horizontal line to show the position of the tops of the eyes. Sketch a horizontal line from the hairline about one-sixth of the way down from the top of the oval. Divide the area below that into three equal parts. The first line below the hairline is for the eyebrows, and the next line shows the location of the tip of the nose. Divide the area below the nose into three more equal parts. The line below the nose is for the mouth opening, and the next line is for the lower lip.

Draw a curved line from the lower right side of the head to show the shape of the neck and backbone. Use rectangles for the chest and hip areas. Draw a curved line between the rectangles for the waist. Form the arms and legs with curved tube shapes. Sketch oval shapes for the shoulders and kneecap. Draw two odd-shaped rectangles for the hands. Use wedge shapes for the feet.

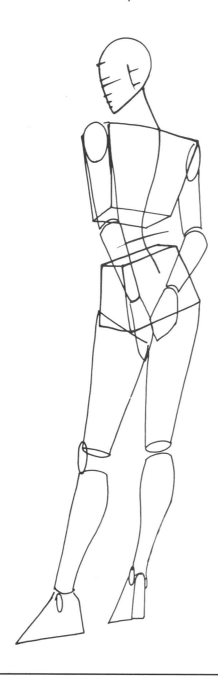

*For each step, draw lightly with your pencil.*

**2** Draw an oval for the ear and extend uneven lines from it to form the hairline. Sketch the neck and shoulders with curved lines. Add full sleeves and a skirt outline with long straight lines. Block the right shoe.

*Use a pen on the final drawing; then erase pencil marks.*

# Woman in a Cocktail Dress continued

**3** Use curved lines to shape the hair. Outline the profile with an uneven line. Draw a curve for the eyebrow and a triangle for the eye. Add a squiggle to the ear. Use two long bent lines for the back of the dress. Sketch odd-shaped triangles and ovals for the bow. Add several straight lines for the folds. Sketch the fingers as shown. Draw a stem with leaves and a rose shape for the flower. Add some straight lines to the back of the skirt for folds. Sketch the shoes with odd shapes.

*For each step, draw lightly with your pencil.*

**4** Add eyelids with small V-shaped figures. Shape full lips using odd-shaped ovals. Draw a bow in the hair with three triangles. Add hair to the back of the neck with wavy lines. Sketch straight and zigzag lines for wrinkles, pulls, and folds on the dress. Crinkle the sleeves with squiggles. Use curved lines to make the peplum hem uneven. Define the flower with curved lines.

*Use a pen on the final drawing; then erase pencil marks.*

# Woman in a Cocktail Dress continued

**5** Shade the hair and bow with squiggles. Add shading to the back of the dress and right ankle. Draw in the veins of the leaves with short straight lines.

*For each step, draw lightly with your pencil.*

# Woman in an Evening Dress

1 Sketch an oval for the head. Divide the oval into left and right halves with a vertical line to determine the center of the face. Separate the oval into upper and lower halves with a horizontal line to show the position of the tops of the eyes. Sketch a horizontal line for the hairline about one-sixth of the way down from the top of the oval. Divide the area below that into three equal parts. The first line below the hairline is for the eyebrows, and the next line shows the location of the tip of the nose. The ears lie between the eyebrows and the nose.

Divide the area below the nose into three more equal parts. The line below the nose is for the mouth opening, and the next line is for the lower lip.

Draw a curved line under the head to show the shape of the neck and backbone. Use rectangles for the chest and hip areas. Sketch a line between the two rectangles for the waist. Form the arms and legs with curved tube shapes. Sketch oval shapes for the shoulders and kneecap. Draw a long oval for the left hand and two triangles for the right hand. Use wedge shapes for the shoes.

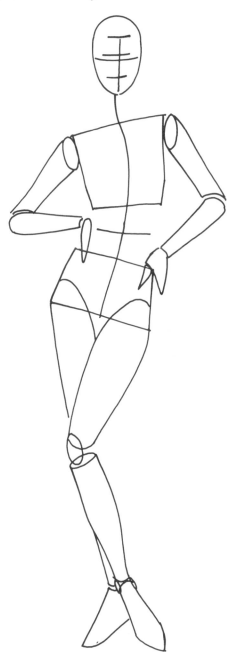

# Woman in an Evening Dress continued

**2** Draw an oval for the ear. Use curved lines for the hairline. Sketch a U-shaped figure for the jawline. Extend a long curved line below the jawline for the neck, shoulders, and arms. Shape the dress with long straight and curved lines.

*For each step, draw lightly with your pencil.*

**3** Draw two curves for the eyebrows and two ovals with pointed ends for the eyes. Shape the nose with straight lines. Add a full mouth by using odd-shaped ovals as shown. Block the hair using long wavy lines. Add a line to the chin and one to the collarbone for definition. Sketch two curves for the neckline and one long curved line for the side of the dress. Shape the shoes with bent lines.

*Use a pen on the final drawing; then erase pencil marks.*

# Woman in an Evening Dress continued

**4** Finish the eyes with darkened ovals. Form the eyelids with curves. Heighten the hair with a wavy line. Add a line to the bottom lip for definition. Sketch a long oval earring with squiggles inside it. Block long gloves with many short lines for folds and wrinkles. Use long straight lines to add a flower shape to the center of the dress. Extend them to show pulls and folds.

*For each step, draw lightly with your pencil.*

**5** Finish the hair with squiggles. Add more shading to the dress and gloves with short straight lines. Detail the flower with curves.

*Use a pen on the final drawing; then erase pencil marks.*

# Bride

1 Sketch a tipped oval for the head. Divide the head into uneven left and right halves with a vertical line to determine the center of the face. Separate the oval into upper and lower halves with a horizontal line to show the position of the tops of the eyes. Sketch a horizontal line for the hairline about one-sixth of the way from the top of the oval. Divide the area below that into three equal parts. The first line below the hairline is for the eyebrows, and the next line shows the location of the tip of the nose. The ears lie between the eyebrows and

the nose. Divide the area below the nose into three more equal parts. The line below the nose is for the mouth opening, and the next line is for the lower lip.

Draw a straight line under the head to show the shape of the neck and backbone. Use a rectangle for the chest area. Form the arms with curved tube shapes. Sketch oval shapes for the shoulders. Draw a big bell shape for the dress. Form the bouquet with an egg-shaped figure between the two hands.

*For each step, draw lightly with your pencil.*

**2** Draw a small oval for the ear. Use curved lines for the hairline and jawline. Block the headpiece with two leaf-shaped figures. Extend two curved lines from the jaw to form the neck. Use curved lines to form the full sleeves. Shape the waist with curved lines. Draw a line across each arm to form a sleeve.

# Bride continued

**3** Draw the eyebrows with short curves. Use two small ovals with pointed ends for the eyes. Sketch the nose with straight lines. Draw the mouth with curved lines as shown. Outline the hair with long curved lines. Shape the headpiece with zigzag lines. Add a small curved line to the neck. Draw a U-figure for the neckline. Form the flowers in the bouquet with odd-shaped circles and ovals. Add some folds to the lower part of the skirt to make the hem uneven.

*For each step, draw lightly with your pencil.*

**4** Add the veil with curly lines. Detail the headpiece with squiggles. Sketch straight and curved lines for the stand-up collar. Add many curved lines to show wrinkles on the dress. Draw two oval lines to define the bodice. Use odd shapes and lines for the flowers.

*Use a pen on the final drawing; then erase pencil marks.*

# Bride continued

**5** Finish the hair with squiggly lines. Add lace to the headpiece and the dress with curly lines as shown. Draw crisscross lines on the veil for texture. Add some small circles on the veil for beading.

*For each step, draw lightly with your pencil.*